# RICHBOROU
## AND
# RECULVEF

KENT

## Susan Harris

*Today, first impressions of the imposing twin towers of the medieval church at Reculver, and the remains of the solid military walls at Richborough, suggest sites with very different histories. However, this is not the case, as both were both Roman settlements that grew up around harbours at either end of the busy Wantsum Channel in the first and second centuries. The Roman remains at Richborough are more extensive: here many ruined buildings and hundreds of thousands of important finds testify to a thriving town and port. With the help of the guidebook tour, the remains of many parts of the Roman fort can also be traced at Reculver.*

*Both sites were later converted into fortified bases in the third century, forming part of a chain of defences around the south and east coasts. When the Romans left, the forts were adapted as early churches, and within the later ruins at Reculver lie the remains of one of Kent's earliest churches, part of a monastery founded in AD 669.*

*This handbook gives a tour and history of each site. Because much of the 'History of Richborough' is also relevant to Reculver, the 'History of Reculver' is briefer and more specific to the site.*

To help you orientate yourself during your visit to Richborough, you can either refer to this bird's-eye painting, or the numbered plan inside the back cover. The numbered points correspond to the location of information panels around the site, and are also given in the written Tour to help link what is on site with both the guidebook text and the plan.

# ❖ CONTENTS ❖

*Published by English Heritage, 23 Savile Row, London W1S 2ET*
*Visit our website at* **www.english-heritage.org.uk**
*Edited by Louise Wilson. Designed by Pauline Hull. Print production by Richard Jones.*
*Printed by Snoeck-Ducaju & Zoon*
© *English Heritage 2001  First published by English Heritage 2001, reprinted 2002*
*ISBN 1 85074 765 2  02782 C30  03/02*
*Photographs by Jonathan Bailey, English Heritage Photographic Unit and*
*copyright of English Heritage, unless otherwise stated.*

# TOUR OF RICHBOROUGH

The route around the site follows a chronological path so that the visible remains are relevant to the history of the site. The most striking features are the high walls of the late third-century fort, but most of what you will see is earlier in date. It can therefore be helpful to try not to think about these walls for the early part of your tour until your attention is specifically drawn to them.

*Interior of the Roman fort showing the early fortified ditch system to the west*

# ❖ THE WANTSUM CHANNE

The geography of this area of Kent was very different in Roman times. The Wantsum, a sea channel up to three miles wide in places, cut off the Isle of Thanet from the mainland with Richborough at the southern edge and Reculver to the north. This was an important passage for ships, providing a stretch of calm water between the east coast and the Thames estuary. The alternative route around Thanet bypasses North Foreland (near Broadstairs) where today a lighthouse stands warning ships off the rocks. This is not an easy stretch of water to navigate as the currents are constantly changing and the water is shallow.

The Wantsum was a busy channel for trade and travel, and was used long before the Romans arrived, and by subsequent generations. The vast amounts of archaeology on the edges of the waterway, dating from the Bronze Age through to medieval times, are an indication of the large numbers of people who lived here before the Wantsum silted up. Until the Romans arrived and built roads, nearly all transport was by water. Even with roads, ships would have been extensively used, as the most economical method using only a tenth of the energy needed overland.

The finds also indicate the wealth of the inhabitants who probably collected tolls from the passing ships. When the Romans arrived Richborough was virtually an island, surrounded on three sides by the sea. Shingle banks to the East, at Stonar, provided a natural harbour, but later helped the channel to silt up. This

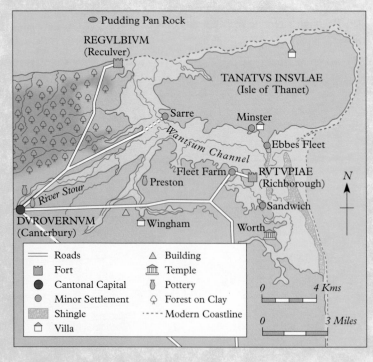

*Map to illustrate the Roman coastline and Wantsum Channel*

*Ancient map of North-east Kent and Thanet (*Antiquatates Rutupiae*) showing Richborough and Reculver at either end of the Wantsum Channel*

process happened over centuries, and it is thought that Richborough was still accessible by boat in the late Saxon period. The central portion of the channel did not close up so quickly, partly due to the river Stour, and in the sixteenth century Henry the Eighth was reputed to have sailed his ships as far as Canterbury. One of the last large vessels known to have navigated the Wantsum was the ship carrying the bells for St. Clements' church in Sandwich down from London in the seventeenth century.

*As you leave the shop, turn right to pass through the break in the wall ahead of you, and find the information panel on the left, 1.*

Pausing here it is worth considering what this area would have looked like when the Romans invaded nearly 2000 years ago. The low-lying land to your right was once part of the Wantsum Channel, a passage of seawater that cut the Isle of Thanet off from the mainland. The sea is now over two miles away, but on a clear day the white cliffs at Pegwell Bay can be seen, with the port of Ramsgate beyond. When the Romans arrived in AD 43, Richborough was surrounded on three sides by the sea, making it practically an island, and had a good natural harbour.

*Three first-century Roman brooches found at Richborough.*

*Now move across the site to the left towards the next information panel, **The Roman Bridgehead, 2.***

## Early defences (AD 43)

The section of twin ditches ahead and to the right of you are the first physical remains of the successful Roman invasion of AD 43, ordered by the Emperor Claudius, and led by the Roman general Aulus Plautius. Forty thousand Roman troops are reputed to have landed here, on the south-east coast, and the parallel ditches are just a small section of an initial defence, which has been traced across the whole

*General plan of Richborough Roman fort and its surroundings*

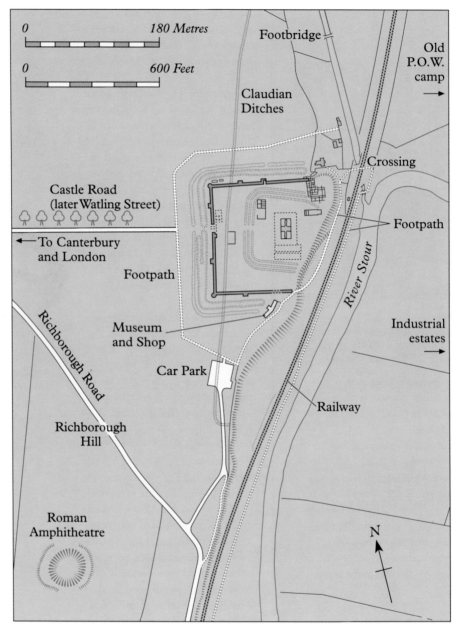

0   180 Metres

0   600 Feet

Footbridge

Old P.O.W. camp →

Claudian Ditches

Crossing

Castle Road (later Watling Street)

Footpath

← To Canterbury and London

River Stour

Footpath

Museum and Shop

Industrial estates →

Richborough Road

Car Park

Railway

Richborough Hill

Roman Amphitheatre

N

area of the high ground on which Richborough stands. An earth rampart would have been built up on the east side of the ditches, nearest the harbour, and a timber palisade with a gateway and possibly a lookout tower near this point. These defences protected the troops and their fleet from any potential threat from the native Britons.

## The supply base (AD 45–85)

*Look to your right towards the centre of the site where rectangular concrete markings are visible on the ground.*

These show the outlines of timber buildings, which formed part of the military and naval supply base and contained the supplies needed for the troops moving further into Britain. They were built after the ditches had been filled in and levelled in about AD 45. The defences had proved unneccessary, as the invading Roman army met with little or no resistance in this area of Kent, and had established a safe harbour. The main east-west road, or *via praetoria*, which led out of the early fort, had surfaced roads to the north and south, breaking up the depot into a grid pattern. The buildings to the south of the main road were storehouses or granaries, and on the north side probably open-fronted shops or stores.

*Look in front of the panel at the concrete markings in the area between the wall and the double ditches.*

This is an outline plan of one of the timber shops or store buildings which was open at the front with a veranda on its south and east sides. The circles show where the timber uprights of the colonnade would have stood.

*Now walk about 50 metres to your right, crossing the triple ditches and climbing the steps to the information panel, **The supply base, 3**.*

The view from this point in the middle of the first century would have been of the crossroads near the centre of the supply depot, with timber buildings on either side. Ahead lay the Wantsum Channel and, it is thought, to the left the Roman harbour, beyond the point where the north wall of the later fort ends. Just inside the wall and to the north-east of the central road is a courtyard building belonging to this period. Known as a

*The interior of the Roman fort showing the triple ditches in the south-west section*

*Model of the triumphal arch on display in the site museum*

*View of the cross-shaped base of the Monumental Arch from the west*

mansio, it probably served either as a military headquarters or a seafront hotel for official visitors from other countries. Panel **6** gives more information about this building.

*The next information panel, **The Building of the Monument, 4,** is about 20 metres to your right.*

## The Monumental Arch (AD 85)

From here you can see the central feature of the site, a large cross-shaped platform of flint and mortar with a gravelled area surrounding it. The whole extent of the gravelled area is in fact a foundation of flints and cobbles set in stiff clay, on which stood a massive triumphal arch, twenty-five metres high. It was clad in white Carrara marble imported from Italy and decorated with bronze statues. The arch crowned the symbolic gateway to the new Roman province of Britannia, and would have been visible for miles around. This impressive monument might have reminded visitors upon arrival that they were entering a civilised part of the Empire. The placing of the arch here emphasises the importance of the site since Richborough (known as *Portus Rutupiae*) had by this time become established as the main entrance port. The archway, straddling the main east-west road, also stood at the start of Watling Street, the Roman road leading to London and then to Chester in the North West.

All that remains of this great archway is the foundation on which it stood and the base of the cross-shaped internal passageways. Evidence suggests that there were marble paved steps leading up to the walkways and that it had carved decoration, and two inscriptions, of which too little is

left to make any sense of them. Similarly, too few fragments of the bronze metalwork survive to piece together the subject, though evidence suggests that it depicted a sea battle and giant figures of Roman gods.

On the west side of the foundation, part of a stone-lined drain for the north-south road can be seen.

*Now walk around the base of the monument to the panel on the far side entitled **The Civilian Settlement, 5.***

## Town and port (second century AD)

A busy town rapidly grew around the Monument with new buildings, streets and an amphitheatre. The amphitheatre lies some distance across the fields, although little can be seen of it now.

To your right, just inside the triple ditches (belonging to a later fortification), are the remains of some stone-built shops. These stood on the edge of the main road and were open at the front with smaller rooms behind for storage or accommodation. They were some of the first buildings on the site to be made of stone – most of the others would have been of timber. (The mansio was also rebuilt in stone at this time).

*Walk round to the other side of the triple ditches behind you to the panel entitled **The Mansio, 6.***

## Mansio

The new stone mansio building replaced a timber structure built in the middle of the first century. The new building included a small heated bathroom and another chamber with a concrete floor and plastered walls. By the middle of the second century this was rebuilt with walls of flint and tile in layers, the outline of which can still be seen. A series of rooms, accessed from outer corridors, also appears to have been added at this time.

When the earth fort was constructed in AD 250, the mansio obviously had an important function as the ditches were intentionally cut to avoid it: they can be seen stopping short on the ground to your right.

The highest remains in this area are of a small bath house, built on top of the previous structures after

*The remains of the mansio and bath house in the north-east corner of the site*

*The postern gateway concealed in the north wall of the fort*

*The point where the triple ditches of the earth fort end abruptly to avoid the mansio building (in foreground)*

the site was levelled for the building of the stone fort in AD 275. Its four separate rooms can still be seen and visited by climbing the steps. In the style of most Roman baths of the time they consisted of a changing room (*apodyterium*), cold bath (*frigidarium*), warm room (*tepidarium*), and hot room (*caladarium*).

*Now turn around and follow the ditches westwards to the panel showing* **The Earthen Military Fort 7** *.*

## Earth Fort (c. AD 250)

The dramatic triple ditch that surrounds the great foundation of the monument was cut in the middle of the third century and enclosed just under half a hectare (about one acre). This was part of a phase of major change to the site probably to give extra defence against Saxon pirates who were raiding the south-east coast. The ditches surrounded an earth rampart which

would have had a wooden fortification placed on top of it, similar to Richborough's initial defences, with an entrance on the west side. Many of the buildings in the town were cleared to make space for this structure.

The monumental arch had fallen into disrepair, and was now used as a watchtower, possibly with a beacon on top.

*Keep walking to your right along the inside of the wall and through the hidden gateway on your right. It is worth pausing here to examine the outside of the north wall.*

## Saxon Shore Fort (c. AD 275)

These stone walls are the remains of the first stone fortification to be built at Richborough. The earlier earth rampart with its wooden fort was levelled within twenty-five years of being built, to make way for this larger stone fort. This, the north wall of the fort, was the most vulnerable, as it would have looked out over the mouth of the Wantsum Channel, with the Roman harbour to the right, and needed protection from seaward attack. This may have been why it was constructed using the best stone available.

The wall is well preserved in this area, with some notable features. On your left, inside the postern gate at the south end, a course of tiles runs right through the wall.

*Continue through the gateway and
turn round to examine the north wall.*

The facing stones of limestone, sand-
stone and ironstone are well preserved,
and are distinctively dressed into cubes
or 'ashlar' blocks – a style frequently
used for Roman walls. The whole fort
would have originally been faced in
this way. Along its length, regularly
spaced holes for the scaffold poles
(putlogs) can be seen. To your left
about two thirds of the way along the
wall, a clear line appears in the
masonry and the wall continues from
here at a slightly different angle. This
indicates that two gangs of builders
worked on the wall from different

# ❖ ROMAN BUILDING TECHNIQUES ❖

The walls of
Richborough
fort reveal some good
examples of Roman
building techniques.
Holes can be seen at
regularly spaced
intervals (on the west
wall these are open
all the way through
the width of the wall).
These are where the
horizontal scaffolding
poles would have
been placed and are
known as 'putlog'
holes. The building gangs would
have constructed the wall to a
comfortable working height above
ground level, then placed poles
across the width of the wall. These
poles would have then been built
on (thereby securing them) and
planks would have been laid along

*Detail of 'join' in the north
wall showing where the work
of two different building
gangs met*

the poles as they
stuck out of the wall
to form walkways.
This method was
highly efficient as
the same scaffolding
poles could be used
for work on both
sides of the wall.
When the building
was finished the
poles could be
pulled out and the
holes plugged with
stone. For any later
maintenance work,
the stone plugs could be removed,
the poles pushed back through and
the scaffolding re-erected.

Another frequently used feature
of Roman wall building to be seen
at Richborough is the incorporation
of tile courses. These can clearly
be seen as narrow bands of

terracotta, running horizontally
through the walls. It is thought
that as well as keeping the rubble
and mortar filling level, these
provided essential bands of water
resistance, thereby preventing frost
damage and cracking in the centre
of the walls – in much the same
way as a modern damp course.
Some Roman walls have tiles used
purely as a
decoration,
running along
the face of
the wall
rather
than
through it.

*Diagram
showing
how
Roman
walls,
such as those at
Richborough, were
constructed*

*Detail of the construction technique on the north wall showing the putlog holes, tile courses and the overall chequerboard appearance*

*Carving of a lion's head, known as Queen Bertha's Head, in the back of the postern gateway*

*Right: View along north wall and base of interval tower*

directions, and met here, with their work slightly out of alignment. On one side, a pattern of alternating light and dark stones appears, and the double course of tiles suddenly extends to three, where adjustments had to be made.

Tucked into a niche halfway up the wall, on the back of the gateway, is a very worn sculpture of a lion. This is missing its head, but part of a mane and the crouched hindquarters can be seen. For no known reason this has been called Queen Bertha's Head, and may have been a decorative feature of the wall, but is more likely to have been moved here from another part of the site.

*Move along the outside of the north wall to the information panel **The Saxon Shore Fort, 8.***

From here it is possible to get a sense of how the fort would have looked at the end of the third century. Anyone wishing to attack would first have to cross the double ditches, making themselves an easy target for any missiles. The postern gate is concealed, and well protected from attack by the wall surrounding it. Rectangular interval towers stand between each gateway, and rounded bastions on the corners, from which the outer face of the wall could be defended.

*Move slightly to your right to see the base of the interval tower protruding from the wall.*

This foundation is a solid block of flint and mortar above which the outline of the rest of the tower can be traced. On the face of the wall there are several tile courses which help to incorporate the tower into the main wall. The three large holes above the base may have held the beams for an upper floor, which possibly had a

trapdoor leading to the lower level. The main walls of the fort still stand up to 8m (twenty-five feet) in height and would originally have had parapets and wall walks along the top.

*Keep moving along the wall around the rounded bastion on the corner, and towards the west gate.*

As you approach the base of the first interval tower, on the west wall, look in the corner where the tower joins the fort. The remains of a tile latrine chute can be seen here, which suggests that the tower was hollow, with a toilet on an upper floor.

*Continue walking until you reach the west gate and stand on the wooden footbridge to see the double ditches to the south of it.*

Looking at the double ditches will reveal what is either a Roman mistake or an alteration – the appearance of a third unfinished ditch. This was filled in soon after it was dug, and is probably another example of building gangs working from different directions and failing to meet.

This gateway was the main land entrance to the fort and had twin towers standing on either side of the roadway (Watling Street). These projected outwards like the interval towers. They would have defended the main land entrance, and probably contained guard chambers.

*Walk back into the fort through the west gateway.*

As you pass through, notice the large foundation stones on which one of the towers must have stood, taken from the dismantled arch.

As well as the bath house on top of the former mansio building, two other buildings inside the fort also belong to the late third or early

*The third, unfinished, ditch just outside the fort near the west gateway*

*Below: Tile latrine chute in the west wall*

*View looking out over the west gateway along the line of Roman Watling Street*

*The foundation stones of one of the towers next to the west gateway*

*Above right: Late Roman baptismal font*

*Right: A Roman amphora found at Richborough, now in the site museum*

*The remains of the chapel of St Augustine in the foreground, with the mansio and bath house buildings in the background*

fourth century. These lie on the south side of the main east-west road through the site, and are marked out on raised areas, indicating the much higher ground level before the surrounding earth was removed during the excavations of the 1920s and '30s.

*Turn left and walk along the inside of the wall until you reach steps on your right leading down to a wine cellar.*

Part of an amphora, (a large pottery storage jar) once containing *lumpha*, (Italian wine from the slopes of Vesuvius) was found here during the excavations.

*Continue to follow the walls around to your right until you come to the next information panel inside the north wall, entitled* **Later Use of the Fort, 9.**

In front of you are the remains of a hexagonal baptismal font built of recycled Roman tiles. It is the last visible piece of Roman building on the site and was once attached to a probable timber Christian church constructed in the late fourth century

*Continue along the inside of the north wall to find the remains of the Chapel of St Augustine. This lies to the right of the mansio building, beyond the base of the monumental arch, with panel 10 inside it.*

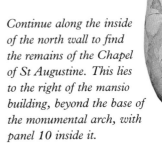

The earliest physical evidence here is of a late Saxon masonry structure with a rectangular chancel. It was more extensively rebuilt in the Norman period with a cemetery to the south now marked out on the ground in concrete. This chapel was in use, (with some alterations and additions), until the seventeenth century.

# HISTORY OF RICHBOROUGH

Richborough is a key site in the history of Roman Britain, used during the entire length of occupation from the invasion of AD 43 to the end of Roman rule in around AD 410. A great deal of activity took place here during this period, as Richborough (or *Rutupiae*, as the Romans called it) developed from an early fortification to a civilian town and port, before returning to military use with the building of a Saxon Shore Fort.

The earliest known inhabitants in this area were the Iron Age Celts, who had farmed the land and left the site before the Romans arrived. Though excavations here between 1922 and 1938 uncovered little evidence of the Iron Age, there was some form of farming settlement abandoned prior to the Roman structures being built. After the Romans left, it appears Richborough saw less activity, though a late Saxon chapel dedicated to St Augustine was built within the walls. As the Wantsum Channel silted up, Sandwich became the main settlement in the area. Apart from its walls being plundered for building stone, Richborough does not seem to have been used again until the twentieth century when it saw military activity in both the first and second world wars.

## The Roman Conquest, AD 43

The history of Richborough therefore really begins with the Roman invasion of Britain in AD 43. The Roman Empire had already established rule in Gaul (modern-day France) and so Britain, an unconquered island on the edge of the Empire, was an ideal conquest for the emperor, Claudius. Before the establishment

*Aerial view of the site from the south-west*

ENGLISH HERITAGE/SKYSCAN BALLOON PHOTOGRAPHY

of Roman rule, Britain was not a unified country but was ruled by separate tribes, and links had been made between some Celtic chiefs and Rome. Other tribes however were opposed to Rome, and there were frequent outbreaks of civil unrest. At this time the *Atrebates* tribe, local to the Sussex area, and allied to Rome, was under threat from its neighbouring tribe, the *Catuvellauni*. When the *Atrebates* appealed to Rome for help, it was the excuse Claudius needed to invade. There were other reasons, including Britain's rich mineral deposits and agricultural land, which made invasion a good economic prospect. Claudius also had a surplus of troops in need of employment, but his main reason for attempting an invasion may have been more personal: he was an unlikely leader who had achieved no great military prowess, and to succeed where his ancestor Julius Caesar had not, might prove his worth as Emperor.

Information relating to the invasion has been pieced together

*Reconstruction drawing by Ivan Lapper of the Roman bridgehead fort as it may have appeared in AD 43*

from archaeological evidence and an account by the Roman historian Dio Cassius, writtten a century and a half later. These sources tell us that the senator Aulus Plautius split the army into three units, and after some delays landed his forces unopposed in Britain and led the invading force. There was no opposition from the Celts, who, confused by the delay in the invasion, had disbanded their forces. Four Roman legions, auxiliary troops and cavalry, totalling over 40,000, therefore invaded without a fight.

Richborough's claim to be the site of the Roman landings in AD 43 has been debated in recent years, but its large bridgehead camp and early supply base make it a strong candidate. At this time Richborough was virtually an island, tidally cut off from the mainland and protected by large shingle banks at Stonar, which provided a sheltered harbour. Its location, close to the Continent, and on the edge of the Wantsum Channel, made it a likely choice. Reculver, at the opposite mouth of the Wantsum, has also produced evidence of Roman activity during this period, which suggests that the Wantsum may have been guarded at both ends as an essential route for moving men and supplies northwards. The Straits of Dover provided the shortest crossing, and followed a route similar to that of Caesar, who landed on the beach between Walmer and Deal nearly a century before.

Having established a safe harbour at Richborough, the Romans created a base camp from which the occupation could progress. This bridgehead fort consisted of double defence ditches (a small section of which can still be seen) with an earth rampart on the seaward side and a wooden palisade along the top. A wooden gateway guarded the entrance to the camp, straddling the main east-west road (later to become the start of Watling Street) which ran across the site and inland towards Canterbury.

The early fort covered a large area: the ditches have been traced for 630m (690yd), and are thought to have run right across the island. These initial defences soon became unnecessary, as there was little resistance to the invasion in this area. By AD 60 the ditches had been filled in and the site levelled, and Richborough saw a new phase of development as a military and naval supply base.

## Flourishing town and port (AD 60-85)

As Roman rule became established throughout the country, the site entered a period of peace and prosperity and began to develop as a flourishing town and port. It was inevitable that Richborough would see a great deal of passing trade as it stood at both road and sea entrances to the new Roman province of Britannia. Equally inevitable was the development of an accompanying

*Steelyard weight in the form of a bearded satyr*

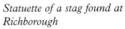

*Statuette of a stag found at Richborough*

town, from the early supply base. The depot, dating from AD 60, was laid out in a grid pattern, with hard surfaced roads dividing the area into blocks. A series of large timber buildings, thought to have been granaries or storehouses, would have contained the supplies vital to the troops as they established roads and settlements, and what are thought to be open-fronted shops have been dated to this period. Untouched by Boudicca's rebellion in AD 60, this area of Kent prospered and in AD 85 Richborough was again cleared for a new town to be laid out around a huge monumental arch.

## Gateway to Britain (AD 85)

The construction of the monument heralded the most significant time for the site. Visible for miles around, and greeting all visitors to the country, it was a lavish political statement, the only known construction of its type built in this country. For any Celtic Briton, who forty years before would have never seen a building larger than a roundhouse, this would have been astonishing. Excavations revealed foundations consisting of a 10m (30ft) deep block of concrete on top of which a raised plinth of stone blocks supported the four-way arch. An estimated 40,000 tonnes of stone,

flint and chalk were needed for the structure which stood to an estimated height of 25m (85ft). Clad in white marble from northern Italy, it carried at least two inscriptions – sadly too little survives to decipher their meaning. Marble columns flanked the four entrances, and giant bronze statues and other bronze decoration crowned the structure. One fragment, the head of a goose, similar in style to those carved on the prows of ships, suggests that a naval battle may have been depicted.

By the second century *Rutupiae* had become an established port, listed on Roman road maps, and famous for its oysters. With the development of Roman rule, many new towns with municipal buildings appeared: locally, *Durovernum* (Canterbury) saw the building of a theatre basilica and forum bathhouse. Richborough had stone buildings added in this period, including shops, and a rebuilding of the mansio which functioned as a 'hotel'. Between the main roads and the monument, timber buildings would have clustered along the streets, and to the south two temples and an amphitheatre served the town. During this time the civilian settlement dominated, and *Rutupiae* as a town and port was at its height. Objects found here tell of the amount of trade which passed

*Left: Decorated Samian bowl*

*Opposite: Part of a reconstruction drawing by Ivan Lapper of the town and port at Richborough*

*Three beakers and a flagon (2nd/3rd century)*

*Right: Flat-sided jug possibly made in France in the late first or second century. Now in site museum*

*Below: Tile fragment with the 'CLBR' (Classis Britannica) stamp*

*The bastion at the south-west corner of the fort*

through from all over the Roman empire, including weights from steelyard balances and amphorae, large pottery containers used for transporting goods such as wine and oil. One amphora was found with a description in ink revealing that the contents – (*lumpha*) was wine from the slopes of mount Vesuvius, with its vintage, weight, producer and shipping agent all noted. Coins were found from as far away as Constantinople and Antioch, also giving a sense of the cosmopolitan nature of the site.

Little evidence survives of the navy having used the site, although a tile stamped CLBR, belonging to the *Classis Britannica* fleet, was discovered which might suggest that the navy had an early base here.

In the first half of the second century, the naval headquarters had moved to Dover, leaving Richborough free of military activity by the mid second century.

## Marauders threaten (AD 250)

Richborough prospered as a town and port until the beginning of the third century when Saxons, Angles and Jutes began to threaten the south and east coasts. The Roman army returned to Richborough to defend the area, and by AD 250 three huge defensive ditches had been dug around the base of the Monument involving the demolition of the central part of the town. The Monument had fallen into disrepair and is thought to have become a lookout tower at the centre of the fortification. The mansio building may by this time have become a headquarters for the new military base.

## Later fortifications (AD 275)

The triple ditch and earth fortifications were soon replaced with a walled fort enclosing a larger area (about eight acres) much of which survives today. This changed the site dramatically, as by AD 275 the town was cleared and the monument pulled down and incorporated into the walls of the fort, emphasising the apparent danger as the symbol of Roman supremacy was destroyed to defend them. The design of the fort was different from those built on Hadrian's Wall in the north of the country in the early second century. It had projecting towers and rounded bastions making it easier to repel attackers. The mansio was demolished with the building of the walls, and a much smaller bath house building was later constructed on the same site at a higher level.

## The Saxon Shore Forts

Richborough was one of a sequence of fortifications whose main purpose is thought to have been to defend against invasion from the Continent, although other ideas about the

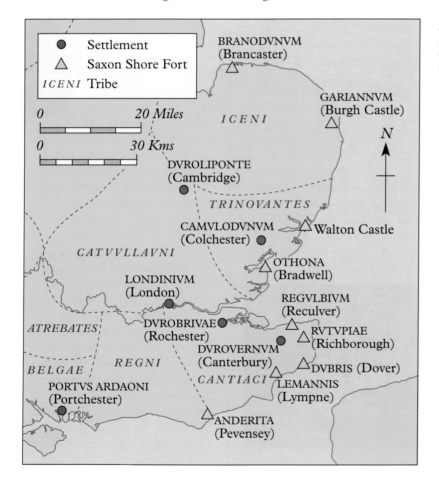

*Map of the Saxon Shore Forts, also showing the divisions between the main Celtic tribal areas*

# RICHBOROUGH'S
# ❖ ROMAN COINS ❖

Some 56,000 coins have been discovered at Richborough during the course of excavations, spanning the entire period of the Roman occupation of Britain (AD 43 to around AD 410). This vast collection tells its own story of the busy port and town which Richborough was, and of the many thousands of people who passed through it. The uniformity of currency throughout the vast Roman empire meant that all people under Roman rule were constantly reminded of their common Emperor by seeing his head on their coins.

Coins were therefore not only used for buying and selling goods, but also for propaganda: some depicted the Empire's victories over barbarian peoples.

Coins can also provide valuable dating evidence for a building or even a specific layer of a building. If a coin of say, AD 123 was discovered in the clay floor of a shop, and, provided there has been no disturbance to that floor (for example, by a later rabbit burrow), then it is known that the earliest possible date for the floor is AD 123. By looking at coins in conjunction with all other forms of dating evidence found during the excavation of a site, such as pottery, radio-carbon dates and the way the layers relate to each other, it may then be possible to give the floor a more specific date, such as mid-second century.

Many forgeries of Roman coins have been found, and there are a number of these in the Richborough collection.

*Above: An* Urbs Romana *coin showing* Romulus and Remus *being suckled by the she-wolf*

reasons for these defences have been put forward. They would certainly have been finished by the time Carausius was appointed by the Emperor Diocletian (AD 286) to put a stop to pirate raids along the Channel coastline of Britain and Gaul. Carausius, a Roman 'admiral,' and commander of the British fleet, is reputed to have maximised his position of power by allowing pirates to pass, and then, on their return, collecting their booty for his own personal wealth. When Roman authorities were informed of this, Carausius had a death sentence pronounced on him, but his position of power was such that he avoided execution, instead declaring himself 'Emperor of Britain'. This position continued until his ex-finance minister, Allectus, murdered Carausius in AD 293. Britain remained a separate empire under Allectus for a further three years before he was defeated by troops from Rome. These events are some of the few recorded in this area during the late third and fourth centuries, although of the 56,000 Roman coins discovered at Richborough, 25,000 of them date from between AD 288 and AD 402, indicating a large amount of activity here during this period. The *Notitia Dignitatum*, an official record dating from the late fourth and early fifth centuries, lists the forts on the south and east coasts, including the legions which were based there. Richborough, housing the legion *II Augusta*, was listed as being one of nine coastal forts under the control of the *Comes Litoris Saxonici* or 'Count of the Saxon Shore'. It is from this entry that the Saxon Shore Forts take their name. Why the word 'Saxon' was used to describe Roman forts is uncertain, though there are two valid views. One is that it referred to the Saxon raiders the forts were built to repel, the other that it was named after Saxon settlers who may already have been here. Archaeological finds do suggest evidence of Germanic occupation at the time the *Notitia* was written.

## The end of the Roman age

By the early part of the fifth century, troops were no longer stationed at the fort, and with the Roman Empire disintegrating along its frontiers, and revolt in Britain, the Roman administration decided that the province would have to look after itself. As the system of Roman rule declined, taxes were no longer demanded, so the towns declined and soldiers were no longer paid.

It seems that the Roman building era did not end with the construction of the fort however,

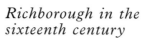

as an early Christian church was uncovered inside the fort walls, with a baptismal font made out of reused Roman tiles. This is thought to have been a timber construction from the late fourth or early fifth century and was probably in use during the last years of the fort's occupation.

After nearly two hundred years, Italians with a very different mission came to this part of Kent, when in AD 597, Pope Gregory sent Augustine to reconvert the English to Christianity. Another chapel, this one belonging to the late Saxon period and dedicated to St Augustine, was built within the walls of the fort, the influence of Rome once again dominating the site.

## Richborough in the sixteenth century

Various historians mention Richborough over subsequent years, one notable visitor being the Tudor writer John Leyland. His account suggests that the church was still in use at this time:

"Within the castle is a little parish church of St Augustine, and an hermitage. I had antiquities of the hermit the which is a industrious man. Not far from the hermitage is a cave where men have sought and digged for treasure. I saw it by candle within and there were no coines. It was so straight that I had no mind to creep far in."

*The Itinerary of John Leyland in or about the Years 1535–1543*

*Stone relief of a Roman goddess thought to have been used as a threshold stone in the early church at Reculver*

*Opposite: Obverse of Roman coin showing the head of Carausius (AD 286–293) found on the site*

*Decorative early first-century oil lamp*

*A gaming board fragment and pieces*

*Roman statuette of Bonus Eventus found on the site*

*Right: Old aerial photograph showing site being excavated in 1928, looking east where the industrial estates are now*

The cave mentioned by Leyland was probably part of the foundation of the monumental arch, as this was hollowed out in one place, much to the interest of later archaeologists.

## Twentieth-century excavations at Richborough

The excavations carried out between 1922 and 1938 led to the most extensive Roman discovery of the twentieth century. Led by J P Bushe-Fox and B W Pearce, they did not benefit from the sophisticated practices in use today, but were at the forefront of contemporary archaeological techniques, and yielded one of the largest Roman collections of artefacts found in Britain. The newspaper cuttings from the national papers report on the 'Exciting New Discoveries' and the 'Mysterious Foundation', revealing the extent to which the finds captured the public imagination. For many years the purpose of the cross-shaped base of the monumental arch eluded the archaeologists, and tunnels were dug to discover any possible entrance to the structure which since Leyland's time, had been thought might contain Roman treasure. The Roman concrete

was set so hard however, that the task was abandoned, and the tunnels left open for visitors to explore, before they became unsafe and were blocked. A light railway ran across the site to remove the spoil, and many local workmen were employed, some of them ex-miners from the nearby coalfields. In August 1938, when the excavations were coming to a close, the site attracted over two thousand visitors. The excavated area was then covered to protect the remains, and was laid out much as it is today.

Displayed on the site are a selection of the Roman finds including everyday objects and domestic items as well as a wide variety of building materials. The small museum holds just a fraction of the objects found here. The majority, including a superb collection of military equipment ranging from the first to the fourth century, are in safe storage, and can be visited for study by prior arrangement.

Since 1984 the site has been in the care of English Heritage.

*The site under excavation in the 1920s*

*Sketch showing excavation in progress in the 1920s to investigate the great foundation of the Monumental Arch*

*Left: The finds shed at Richborough during excavations*

# TOUR OF RECULVER

The most dominant features of the site at Reculver are the medieval towers of the church, which stand out on the skyline for miles

*View of the twin towers from the inside of the church*

around. These belong to the later part of Reculver's history while the first remains to be examined here date from about a thousand years earlier when the Romans occupied the site. The Roman Fort stood about 1km (three quarters of a mile) from the sea. It was positioned at the north end of the Wantsum Channel at the point where the channel joined the Thames Estuary.

## The Roman Fort

Starting from the car park you can see, disappearing behind the inn, the remains of the west side of the Roman fort – a stretch of flint and mortar wall, which is thought to date from the early third century AD.

*To continue along the line of the Roman wall, take the right hand exit out of the car park and follow the path ahead of you, with the caravan park on your right. As you do so look for the portion of Roman wall that appears in the bank on your left.*

*Stop when you notice a break in the vegetation about half way along.*

This was once the south wall of the fort which would have overlooked the Roman harbour, situated where the caravans are now.

The way the wall was constructed can be seen in the regular courses of flint in mortar. The facing stones have not survived but were of small stone blocks. The walls, which once stood up to 4.5m (15ft) high had an earth rampart built up behind them, and would have had a wall walk and parapet on top. They were surrounded by a set of double ditches spaced about 10m (33ft) and 20m (66ft) from the wall. Inside the earth bank a road is thought to have run around the circuit of the fort.

Immediately above this point the south gateway once stood, and its remains can be examined later, from above.

*Continue until you reach the corner where the path turns left, then follow it along the east wall of the fort for about thirty paces.*

*View along the remains of the south wall of the Roman fort*

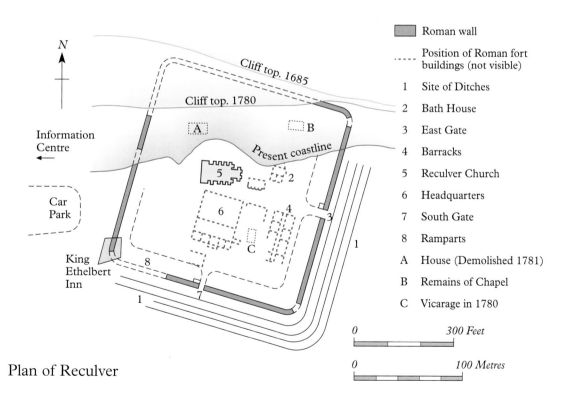

Plan of Reculver

Roman wall

Position of Roman fort buildings (not visible)

1 Site of Ditches
2 Bath House
3 East Gate
4 Barracks
5 Reculver Church
6 Headquarters
7 South Gate
8 Ramparts
A House (Demolished 1781)
B Remains of Chapel
C Vicarage in 1780

*Repair work in the east wall of the fort*

*The base of the guard chamber at the east gate*

A portion of the wall was repaired here soon after it was built, and this can be seen as a distinct bulge in the structure where the regular courses of flints are broken by an area of roughly laid masonry.

*Walk on to where the path leads through a break in the wall to the left.*

This was the east gateway to the fort, which had a single carriageway 2.7m (9ft) wide running through it. A hard surfaced road (the *Via Principalis*) ran across the site from here to the west gate. This entrance had a guard chamber on the north side, the remains of which are still visible, and tiles appear in the construction of the surrounding wall, which is thought to indicate rebuilding. The excavations in this area revealed that the gate was blocked in the late third or fourth century.

*Turning away from the fort, pause here to consider the surrounding area beyond the caravans.*

The east gate would have been roughly half way along the wall here, indicating that nearly half of the fort has fallen into the sea (it once measured 170m by 180m (570 by 600ft), enclosing about eight acres of land). To understand the changes in the landscape of this area since Roman times, one has to consider that much of what was once dry land is now sea, and to the south and east, what was once water has

now silted up and become land. When the fort was occupied, this view would therefore have been very different, overlooking a busy shipping route connecting the Roman port at Richborough with the Thames estuary.

Diagonally to your right (on a clear day) a square church tower can be seen on the horizon at St. Nicholas at Wade. Beyond this, at the opposite end of the Wantsum Channel, are the remains of the Roman fort at Richborough.

*Turn back towards the fort and follow the path into it to a point level with the nearest end of the church.*

The corner of the church nearest to you stands on what was once the centre of the fort. To the south, on the field directly opposite, the excavations revealed a headquarters building, with its entrance facing north, indicating that the main gate to the fort was from the direction of the current coastline. Evidence of several other Roman buildings was also found, including a bath house, and barracks.

*Walk away from the church and across to the far side of the field where the remains of the south gate can be seen.*

The gateway is lower than the field, which has risen in height from the layered remains of years of habitation. It was similar in construction to the east gate, but with its guard chamber to the right, rather than the left, of the entrance (when looking out from inside the fort). The outline is marked out on the ground in concrete and a little of the original construction remains. One large foundation stone has a hole from which the pivot for the gate would have swung.

*Having investigated all the surviving features of the Roman fort, walk back across the field and into the ruins of the church, standing centrally with your back to the towers.*

## The Saxon Church

You are now standing in the nave of the Saxon church, built in AD 669 by the Abbot Bassa. Originally a monastic church, this later became the parish church of Reculver, a small

settlement to the west of the church, situated roughly where the car park is now, and since destroyed by the sea.

The nave is the main body of the building where the congregation would have gathered. Some of the original walls still stand to two metres

*View from between the towers of the layout of the church*

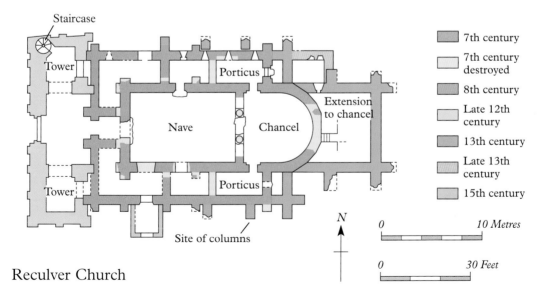

Staircase

Tower

Porticus

Nave

Chancel

Extension to chancel

Tower

Porticus

Site of columns

N

0   10 Metres

0   30 Feet

| | 7th century |
| | 7th century destroyed |
| | 8th century |
| | Late 12th century |
| | 13th century |
| | Late 13th century |
| | 15th century |

# Reculver Church

*The groove around the south porticus entrance where an inlaid band of stone surrounded the doorway*

*Right: Artist's reconstruction of the Reculver Cross (front and back) from the fragments*

*The splayed internal sill of the north window of the Saxon church*

(six feet) in height, while the outline of the others is marked out on the ground in concrete edged with flints. At the rear of the church, nearest the towers, the nave had doorways leading into it from the west and to the north and south for which gaps in the ground plan can be seen.

*Move forward away from the towers until you find two round bases of concrete on the ground.*

These circles marked the position of two columns which once formed the central portion of a triple-arched screen. This decorative partition divided the chancel from the nave. In front of the screen the Reculver Cross is thought to have stood. The two columns of the arch and fragments of the Cross are now on display in Canterbury Cathedral.

On either side of this point where the nave and chancel meet, were small chapels known as porticus. Recycled Roman tiles stand out in the construction of these rooms, which had external doorways to the east.

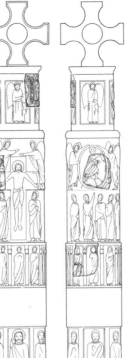

*Look for the following seventh-century features in the porticus.*

To your right, a groove around the entrance to the south porticus can be seen where an inlaid band of stone surrounded the doorway.

On the other side of the chancel, the north chamber is better preserved as it contains more of the original construction, including the remains of two windows, which feature reused Roman tiles. Standing inside this porticus, facing the sea, the lower sections of the right window can be clearly seen with the sill sloping inwards and the sides splaying out. The window to the left is less intact as alterations were made when a wall-mounted tomb was inserted.

*Walk from inside the north porticus towards the towers, stepping over what would have been its rear wall and into the next rectangular 'room'.*

This chamber is one of four rooms added to the west end of the church at this time, on either side of the nave.

Beyond this room, nearer to the towers, other L-shaped extensions were added, thereby extending the church to where the later towers begin. The missing areas are indicated with broken flint on the surface of the concrete markings, to distinguish it from the earlier ground plan of concrete edged with flint. The other features of this period are the external buttresses supporting the walls, which can be clearly seen on both north and south sides.

The addition of the towers was the next change, when a series of alterations were made at the end of the twelfth century – the first substantial developments to take place in over four hundred years. The walls dividing the rooms on either side of the nave would have been demolished to create a pair of aisles. Looking at the towers from inside the church, the sloping lines of the original roof can be traced. The tower nearest the sea has a staircase leading to three floors above and a walkway between the towers can be reached from the first floor.

The towers themselves had a new west doorway between them, now blocked, which would have been highly decorated with carved stonework surrounding the entrance; they also had wooden spires as can be seen from the engraving by the Buck brothers (1781) on p33.

*Follow the outside of the north wall, nearest to the sea, away from the towers, and back to the east end of the church. Pause when you reach the remains of a chamber level with the eastern end of the Saxon chancel.*

This small porch entrance was not enclosed until the late thirteenth century; the remains of worn steps can be seen leading into the extended chancel beyond.

*Make your way into the centre of the chancel and stand with your back to the towers.*

This large rectangular chancel, added in the thirteenth century when the aisles were extended and rebuilt, had a triple window facing east, decorated with Purbeck marble columns. To your left the stonework which once supported the arch of a double window can be seen high up on the wall giving an impression of the scale of the building.

*The last view of the church is from the outside of the towers. As you leave the church, notice the gravelled area leading out from the nave, which marks the position of a porch added in the fifteenth century.*

The west doorway between the towers was once decorated with ornately-carved stonework and flanked by columns with Purbeck marble capitals. The bases of these columns still remain by the doorway, which once greeted generations of worshippers from the parish beyond.

*The church roofline visible on the inside of the tower*

*Above: The worn steps leading from the north porch to the chancel*
*Below: The blocked west doorway between the towers*

# HISTORY OF
# RECULVER

## Roman Reculver

Archaeological discoveries suggest
that Reculver, like Richborough, may
have served as a small initial camp
and safe harbour for the invading
Roman force under the Emperor
Claudius in AD 43. Excavations have
also revealed older material, including
evidence of an Iron Age farmstead.

Early military ditches were
discovered at Reculver (or *Regulbium*
as the Romans called it) enclosing
about half a hectare (an acre) of land
with an earth rampart and timber
palisade barrier. This is likely to have
served as an initial camp and safe
harbour for a small part of the
invading force. More information
about the Roman invasion can be
found on pages 5 to 6 and 15 to 17,
in the part of the guidebook dealing
with Richborough, as this early Roman
history is relevant to both sites.

It is thought that a settlement was
established to the north and west of
the current fort, as the remains of
wells have indicated occupation in the
second and third centuries. The
Roman community at Reculver
would probably have covered a larger
area than the later fort.

The walled fort, dating from the
first half of the third century, possibly
as early as AD 210, is similar in style
to earlier forts in the north of the
country on Hadrian's Wall. It was
almost square – 170 by 180m (570
by 600ft) with rounded corners and
no external bastions – and would
have overlooked the harbour to the
south and the mouth of the Wantsum
Channel beyond. The early date of
this fort is unusual and raises
questions about the purpose of the
fortification at this time, since the
majority of the south and east coast
was not defended until the latter half
of the third century. Reculver
certainly became one of the series of
defences later known as the Saxon
Shore Forts, but its initial purpose
may have been different. One other
Roman fort, contemporary with
Reculver, and of a similar design, is

at Brancaster in Norfolk. Because of the early date of these two forts it has been suggested that the east coast was in need of protection from pirates before the south coast which was patrolled by the Roman navy, the *Classis Britannica*. For more information about the Saxon Shore Forts see the history of Richborough (pages 10 to 12).

Excavation work carried out inside the fort revealed a barracks, bath houses and a headquarters building whose entrance faced north. This indicates that the main gate to the fort was on the north side facing the sea. This headquarters building (*principia*) contained a most exciting find: a strong room was uncovered containing pieces of an inscription, which provides some clues to the date of the building. The fragments refer to Rufinus, the governor of Britain when the *principia* and *basilica* were constructed. Although it is not certain when Rufinus was governor, it is thought that he was in office during the third century, which helps to date the construction.

One other source of information referring to Reculver is the *Notitia Dignitatum*, a document which lists the forts under the command of the 'Count of the Saxon Shore', and the units which were posted at them during the late fourth century.

*Eighteenth-century engraving of Reculver Church from the south by Samuel and Nathaniel Buck*

THE SOUTH VIEW OF RECULVER-ABBY, IN THE COUNTY OF KENT.

To Sᵣ EDWARD DERING Barᵗ Knight of the Shire for the County of Kent. This Prospect is most humbly Inscrib'd by his much Oblig'd humble Servᵗ Samˡ & Nathˡ Buck.

THIS Abby was built A.D. 669 (on the Site whereon a Roman Garrison stood) by Basia a Priest, who procur'd the Place from Egbert King of Kent, & was annex'd to Christ Church in Canterbury by King Eadred, but continued a Monastery till Egelnoth was Archbishop of Canterbury, who converted y Abbacy into a Deanery. Ethelbert King of Kent in the Saxon Heptarchy removing from Canterbury fixt his Palace here. The chief Remains of this Antique Building are y Towers, of great use to Seamen for avoiding Sands & Shelves in the Mouth of the River Thames. S & N Buck delin et sculp 1735.

*The two seventh-century columns from the Saxon church, now in the crypt of Canterbury Cathedral*

*Fragment from the Reculver Cross now on display in Canterbury Cathedral*

At Reculver the *Cohors I Baetasiorum* is listed as the garrison based at the fort, a unit previously stationed at Maryport in Cumbria in the late second century. It is thought that this unit may have been the one involved in constructing the fort; tiles have been uncovered stamped with the initials CIB, and the similarity in style with the earlier northern forts lends weight to this theory.

Reculver has produced little evidence of occupation in the fifth century – the last regular garrison to have been stationed there would have been withdrawn by the end of the fourth, and as Roman control of Britain gradually ceased, the fort seems to have been deserted.

## Christian history of Reculver

After the Romans left, Reculver became a royal estate, and remained so until Egbert, the King of Kent, granted the land to Bassa for the foundation of a monastery in AD 669, with a church dedicated to St. Mary the Virgin. This consisted of a simple nave for the congregation, and a semi-circular chancel, divided from each other by a screen of three arches formed out of two stone columns and re-used Roman tiles. These columns, over 4.2m (14ft) in length and made of Marquise limestone from Calais, were initially lost in the nineteenth-century demolition, but were found in an orchard in the late nineteenth

century and today can be seen in the crypt of Canterbury Cathedral.

Also preserved in the Cathedral are fragments of the Reculver Cross, which is recorded to have stood at the end of the nave, in front of the arcade. This feature has been dated from between the seventh and ninth centuries and was still standing when the historian John Leland visited the site in 1540. He wrote that this, 'the fairest and most auncyent crosse' was 2.7m (9ft) high, the cross crowning a round pillar decorated with carved figures representing the Apostles and the Ascension of Christ. By the end of the seventh century, Reculver had achieved a high reputation, as the then Abbot Britwald (Berhtwald) became Archbishop of Canterbury. The original Saxon Church was extended in the eighth century and owned the surrounding land as far as Herne and St. Nicholas at Wade, with a significant income.

During the ninth century, successive Viking raids plundered the Isle of Sheppey, Rochester and Canterbury, and, in AD 850, the Vikings returned and camped on the Isle of Thanet posing a continuous threat to the monastic community at Reculver.

In the following years this area of Kent was ransacked and all the monasteries in the area were abandoned. Little of Reculver's history survives from this period, and in AD 949 it was handed over to the Archbishopric of Canterbury.

# ❖ DOMNEVA'S DEER ❖

When Augustine arrived to reintroduce Christianity in AD 597, Ethelbert, the King of Kent, became a convert and gave Augustine the royal residence in Canterbury so that a Cathedral could be founded. Legend has it that Ethelbert then moved his court to Reculver, which continued as a royal estate until AD 669. At this time, Ethelbert's great-grandson, Egbert, handed the site over to Abbot Bassa for the foundation of a monastery. King Egbert is said to have been responsible for the murder of his two cousins and the gift of Reculver, for the founding of a monastery, was by way of atonement for this.

The murder had wider repercussions, as Queen Ermenburga (or Domneva), the sister of the murdered brothers, arrived from Mercia to claim 'wergeld', the financial compensation traditionally awarded for this kind of loss. Rather than money however, Domneva requested a portion of land, the size of which was to be decided by the course of her tame deer, which she set free to wander across the Isle of Thanet and thereby established a boundary. She then founded a convent at Minster, on

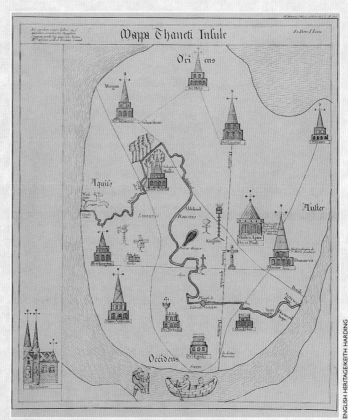

*This early map of the Norman churches in the area unusually places east at the top, and shows the course of Domneva's deer running across the Isle of Thanet*

ENGLISH HERITAGE/KEITH HARDING

Thanet, so that prayers could be said for the souls of the murdered brothers. The Abbey of Minster in Thanet is contemporary with Bassa's church at Reculver, dating from 670, and is just a few miles away. Thanet has Domneva's deer as its symbol to this day.

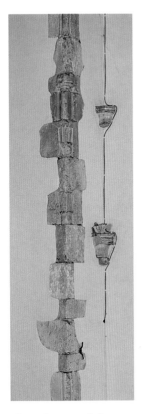

*Carved stonework from Reculver church, re-used in the church at Hillborough*

Reculver then became a parish church, and in the twelfth century it was extended with the addition of the towers. The towers were supposedly intended to aid ships navigating the coastline and were reputedly added at the request of a prioress from Davington, near Faversham, who was saved from being drowned nearby.

In the thirteenth century the chancel was extended and wooden spires placed on the towers; porches were added later in the fifteenth century.

To the west of the church a substantial settlement had grown up over the years, but the gradual erosion of the coastline meant that its residents began to abandon it, moving instead to Hillborough. Leyland reported the sea to be a quarter of a mile from the church in 1540, and by 1781 the north-west corner of the fort had fallen away. After the rapid destruction of some nearby houses, the vicar persuaded his parishioners to demolish the building, and in 1809 this was completed using gunpowder to blow up the walls.

Much of the stone from the church was re-used in building a new church at Hillborough, although some was sold for the construction of Margate pier. The towers were left standing and were bought by the maritime corporation, Trinity House, for £100 as a navigation aid, before the site was put in the care of the Ministry of Works in 1925. Substantial work has gone into the sea defences over the years to ensure that no further erosion takes place.

Reculver played a more recent role in military history as the location for the 'Dam Busters' bomb trials during the Second World War. This point on the coast was chosen for the shallowness of the sea here, which meant that objects could easily be recovered from the vast expanse of mudflats exposed at low tide.

Since 1984 the site has been in the care of English Heritage.

## Acknowledgements

Dr Stephen Johnson
Alan Ward
Keith Harding (for kind permission to photograph and reproduce the early maps on Pages 5 and 35.)
Brian Philp, without whose research at Reculver the text relating to this site could not have been written.

## Key sources

Johnson, S.1997 *Richborough and Reculver*
Johnson, S. 1979 *The Roman Forts of the Saxon Shore*
Johnston, DE ed.1977 *The Saxon Shore*, Council for British Archaeology Research Report No. 18
Philp, B. 1986 *The Roman Fort at Reculver*
Maxfield, VA ed. 1989 *The Saxon Shore*.